HOW TO 'K
AND OTHER OVERTONE SINGING STYLES

HOW TO 'KHÖÖMEI'
AND OTHER OVERTONE SINGING STYLES

Jonathan Cope

With thanks to the peoples of
Tuva and Mongolia

Published by Wild Wind & Sound For Health.
www.soundforhealth.com
e-mail to Info@soundforhealth.com

Printed by Oxuniprint, Oxford University Press.

Illustrations, design, and layout by Jonathan Cope.

CONTENTS

INTRODUCTION

Increasing numbers of people are finding themselves drawn to the ethereal and intriguing sounds that have travelled into Europe and America, primarily from Mongolia and Tuva in the former Soviet Union. Most recently popularised in the West by the touring musicians Huun Huur Tu, Yat Kha, and Sainkho Namatchlyak this fascinating style* of singing allows the simultaneous production of two or more notes by the same singer. This astounding feat is accomplished by deliberate enhancement of the natural harmonics found in our voices. The voice, mouth, lips, teeth, jaw, throat, tongue, lungs and diaphragm can all be used in a subtle and complex concert that will allow you to produce these wonderful sounds. This book will lead you through the whole process in easy-to-follow sections with plenty of illustrations, whilst the enclosed CD will allow you to hear the sounds you should be making at each stage.

*Actually many styles, as we will see.

A BRIEF OVERVIEW AND HISTORY

The title of this book mentions the name 'khöömei'. It is worth pointing out that few people can agree on exact spellings and definitions. In Mongolia and Tuva it is known as xöömii or xöömij (variously translated as 'throat', 'pharynx' or 'guttural'). More recently, in the West, the spelling 'khöömei' seems to be most used. This term has been used as a 'catch-all' name for many styles of singing which have become known as throat singing, overtone singing, or harmonic singing. I wrote this book to be of real practical use to anyone interested in learning to sing in this way so I do not intend to dwell on the various definitions or physics of the whole process too much. If, after reading this book you wish to know more about the background or physics of throat singing you could try some of the excellent (albeit rare and hard to find) books mentioned in the resource section at the end.

As Western styles of throat singing differ from those used in Central Asia I will use the term 'overtone singing' to describe the Western styles and 'khöömei' for the Eastern. In Central Asia (Mongolia and Tuva primarily) 'khöömei' is used as a 'catch-all' for all types of throat singing, but is also a distinct style amongst others. Other peoples and cultures have derivations of this type of polyphonic (or multi-note) singing; 'umngqukolo' in the Xhosa tradition of South Africa, the 'One voice chord' or 'Yang' deep chant of the Tibetan Buddhist monks, and also other types from peoples of the Inuit or 'Eskimo' cultures. Something akin to the multi-note singing (that characterises all the styles of 'throat' singing) exists in the West but is produced by the interaction of two or more people; liturgical chanting in Sardinia, Gregorian chant, and other 'close harmony' styles like American Barbershop singing.

It is believed that forms of khöömei have existed in Central Asia for many hundreds (possibly thousands) of years. It was typically sung by shepherds from many of the nomadic tribes in this region, who used it to imitate the sound of the wind in the mountains. Many of these cultures have a strong tradition of shamanic / animistic beliefs and imitate many of the sounds of nature heard around them to 'praise' good nature spirits or ward off evil ones. Nowadays the nomadic life is giving way to city and urban cultures so the newest khöömei singers are more likely to be young men with motorbikes rather than horses. Although traditional songs are having a renaissance, younger singers often enjoy using forms of khöömei with rock & roll or punk songs. The first field recordings of traditional khöömei were made in the 1930's and by the 50's and 60's these had started to catch imaginations in the West. The popularisation of overtone singing in the West is due in part to the German avant-garde composer Karlheinz Stockhausen, who used it in his 1967 piece 'Stimmung'. In addition, Tran Quang Hai, a Vietnamese ethnomusicologist and multi-instrumentalist based in Paris, has done much since the late 60's to teach and lecture on all styles of throat singing, including the Central Asian styles.

Although relatively new to the West, overtone singing has caught the attention of many groups of people for different reasons. Those studying phonetics (the study of speech production) have been intrigued by the physical aspects of the various techniques used in the production of overtones and how they relate to the formation of the spoken word. Specialists in the field of ear, nose and throat medicine have also studied the techniques in order to understand the processes involved and to discern whether any cultural genetic physiology was involved (they concluded no specific physiology was required and that the techniques could be learnt by all). Musicians and singers have been drawn to the wonderful and unique sounds that can be produced when throat singing, and also the fact that the tones produced follow the overtone series so perfectly. Practitioners and therapists working within complementary medicine and the healing arts have discovered that these unique sounds can have a profound effect on mind and body, whilst the general public has responded to overtone singing often with disbelief that such sounds are produced by the human voice. The unifying factor seems to be that, on hearing throat singing / overtone singing for the first time, the reaction is one of 'Wow! – how is that possible?', closely followed by 'How can I do that too?'. These were definitely personal reactions on my first exposure to this new sonic world and it is my humble hope that this book will aid your fulfilment of the goal to make these amazing sounds too.

HARMONICS AND OVERTONES

Almost all sources of musical notes produce overtones. Only the pure tones of things like computer synthesisers and tuning forks are able to produce a musical note that is devoid of overtones. Most musical instruments, the human voice included, carry many other tones on top of the desired note – these are the overtones. Also called harmonics and partials, they add colour and timbre to the sound. These terms are ways to describe the way in which many sounds do not have just one pure note but also many other subtle notes at different pitches and intensities. It is the presence of harmonics in sounds that render them so unique to their source – be that a cello, a flute, an aeroplane, or the human voice. Harmonics help shape the spoken word, differentiate the voices of individuals, and are also the building blocks of what we perceive as regional or national dialects. Harmonics colour the sonic landscape of our world.

Like most things in existence, sound appears to be governed by underlying patterns. Harmonics appear at regular positions in relation to one another, these positions in turn relate to a series of whole-number ratios. When throat singing the first fixed note (the note we sing) is called the fundamental and each of the overtones appear at whole-number ratios of 2:1, 3:1, 4:1, etc. above this note. To put this another way, if we produce a note of low A (110 Hz (or cycles / vibrations per second)) then the first overtone* will appear at 220Hz, the third at 330Hz, the fourth at 440Hz and so on. In this way the higher overtones quickly move to frequencies that far exceed those capable of being produced by a normal singing voice. D1 shows the pitch of harmonics against loudness. As the harmonics ascend in pitch they get closer together and quieter.

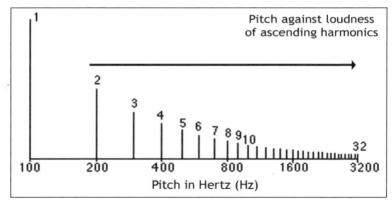

D1

*(Correctly the second harmonic as the first note is harmonic one and notes above these are known as 'overtones' as they are 'over the tone').

Another feature of this pattern is that the higher the

overtones get the closer they are to each other and, therefore, more difficult to isolate and exaggerate. And I'm afraid it gets worse. The physics of acoustics mean that the perceived loudness or strength of the harmonics gets less as they get higher and the loudness of the human voice drops off quite quickly once the sound has exited the mouth. All this conspires against us to ensure that the feat of producing loud, clear, harmonics or overtones high up the scale is really quite extraordinary. Another way of looking at harmonics uses the model of

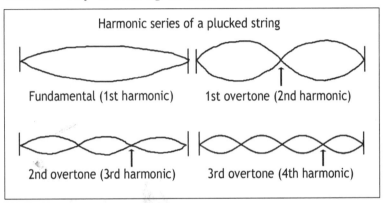

the single string. D2 shows some harmonics on a string that could be on a guitar, cello, etc. When plucked the string will vibrate at a frequency that we hear as a musical note and harmonics or overtones can be found at certain positions along the string.

This discovery was first put forward by the Greek mathematician and philosopher Pythagoras in 6 BC. He found that a single string, when plucked, would yield its second harmonic at exactly half way across the string, i.e. dividing the string into two. This first overtone features a frequency of oscillation twice that of the fundamental, or note first plucked. This can be described as a ratio of 2:1 (two oscillations for each of the original one) which relates to the difference in tone or pitch we call an octave. The next harmonic appears at a position that is a third of the way into the string, i.e. divided into three equal parts, so this is the ratio 3:1, the next at 4:1 (four equal parts), 5:1 (five equal parts), etc. In this way the harmonics get closer together as they ascend the scale because the interval (gap) between successive harmonics becomes smaller and smaller.

Another interesting phenomenon that affects how we look at harmonics or overtones is in the way in which they relate to the Western musical scale. Throughout the history of music different ways of dividing up the series of notes that the human ear can register have been used. We have seen how the difference between a note and the resultant note when the first is doubled in frequency is referred to as an octave. The semitones (part notes) within this octave range have been divided up according to different principles.

Originally the positions were dictated by the natural positions of the harmonics as described above. Unfortunately (from our point of view) in the mid 1800's J.S. Bach proposed a system called even temperament. This system divided the twelve semitones in an octave into positions that had an even multiple between them. This means that the notes on a modern piano do not follow the overtone series and differ from the natural harmonic positions for several of the notes. Therefore you may wish to find the harmonics on a stringed instrument, such as a guitar, as an aid for learning the harmonic series rather than use a piano. Within the system of even tempering the modern Western division of the octave features eight full tones or notes that are referred to as a scale. You may know these as the ascending tones sung as 'do, re, mi, fa, so, la, ti, do', the first and last 'do' are one octave apart. These notes equate to the white keys on a piano between C and C. The black keys in between these eight keys are the 'flatted' notes, of which there are five, to make the total of twelve semitones. If you are familiar with music theory you may find the diagram below useful as it shows the first series of overtones from a C fundamental.

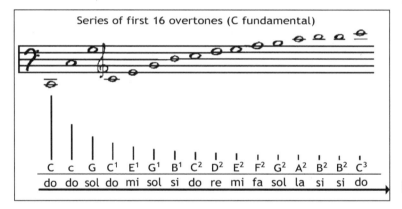

Series of first 16 overtones (C fundamental)

| C | c | G | C¹ | E¹ | G¹ | B¹ | C² | D² | E² | F² | G² | A² | B² | B² | C³ |

do do sol do mi sol si do re mi fa sol la si si do

D3

PHYSIOLOGY OF THE VOICE

Before moving on to the practical sections in earnest it may be helpful to know a little of the structures in the body that we will be using when singing, along with some exercises to help warm up and ensure that no strain is caused whilst practicing. D4 shows the main components of the human head and throat that relate to the production and control of sound. Along with the lungs and diaphragm these structures are able to work together to produce a truly astounding range of sounds. Take a little time to study the position of the various structures and think about how they relate to your own body – you will come to know and feel many of these parts quite profoundly as you learn to throat sing! We will be looking at taking more conscious control over the tongue, the vocal cords, the glottis and the throat itself so it pays to know which is which.

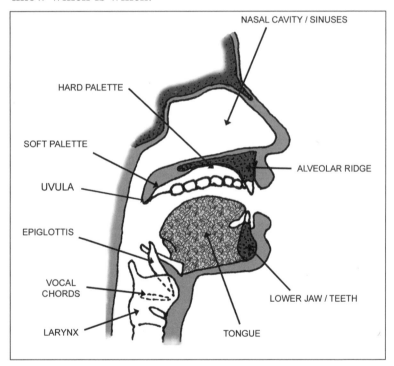

D4

KEY
Alveolar ridge - A short distance behind the upper teeth the angle of the roof of the mouth changes, this is the alveolar ridge. For some people this will have a slightly

ridged feel to it. The tongue tip 'fixes' here for some singing styles.

'Hard' palate - The hard part of the roof of the mouth. This arches up in varying degrees between individuals and some people have a ridge that runs centrally front to back. This ridge is useful for the tongue to follow in some styles of singing.

Soft palate/velum - The soft part of the roof of the mouth, just behind the hard palate. The tongue hits the velum in the consonants 'k', 'g'. The velum can also move: if it lowers, it creates an opening that allows air to flow out through the nose; if it stays raised, the opening is blocked, and no air can flow through the nose. This process makes sounds more or less nasal in quality.

Uvula - That small dangly thing at the back of the soft palate!

Pharynx - The tube consisting of the walls of the upper throat.

Tongue blade - The flat surface of the tongue just behind the tip.

Tongue body - The main part of the tongue. This moves to form the sounds we hear as vowels and many of the consonants.

Tongue root - The lowest part of the tongue in the throat. All parts of the tongue, including the root, will need to be consciously controlled to a high degree to allow the production of overtones.

Epiglottis - The fold of tissue below the root of the tongue which helps cover the larynx during swallowing, making sure that food goes into the stomach and not the lungs.

Vocal folds / vocal cords - These are folds of tissue stretched across the airway to the lungs. They can vibrate against each other and produce sound during speech and singing. Their tension dictates the pitch of an individual's voice. As the voice is raised in pitch, so the vocal cords become tighter.

Glottis - The opening between the vocal cords. The opening and closing of this when speaking is called a 'glottal stop'. This structure is useful for some styles of throat singing.

Larynx - The structure that holds and manipulates the vocal cords. The "Adam's apple" in males is the lump in the exterior throat formed by the front part of the larynx.

Researchers in the field of phonetics (study of the processes of speech production) have found that the human voice naturally uses harmonics to enhance the way we perceive certain vocal sounds. When we speak or sing the diaphragm pushes air from the lungs which then moves up the larynx and through the vocal cords causing them to vibrate. This sound vibration interacts with the structures of the throat and mouth and certain frequencies are naturally enhanced, these are known as formants.

Formants are formed in the throat and find focal points at the back of the tongue, in the roof of the mouth, and at the lips. Formants are linked with vowel production in normal speech and vary between individuals and cultures. However, different vowel sounds will naturally tend to enhance one or two frequencies or harmonics that help give the vowels their characteristic sounds. We can use formants to our advantage, when trying to throat sing, by using vowels as the triggers for different overtone frequencies that we will learn to focus and enhance.

Although voice pitch and harmonic frequencies vary greatly between individuals it has been found that certain vowel sounds naturally enhance a range of frequencies that are pretty uniform.

The vowels may help to trigger the correct range of harmonic frequencies but the extreme fine-tuning that is required to filter them correctly falls to the control of the complex interrelationship between the vocal apparatus and the ear / brain. Tuning your ear into the subtle nature of harmonics will mean that you will become more efficient at finding their starting points and using small changes in lip, jaw, tongue, etc. to focus and filter them to an increasingly fine degree. As you filter the harmonics more efficiently you will be providing the maximum amount of vibrational energy for the production of clear overtones.

Although just about anyone can learn to throat sing we have seen that the nature of harmonics means that they fall within fixed ratio positions from any given fundamental. Raise the pitch of the fundamental and the associated overtones move up with it, this process has been likened to raising a ladder – the rungs stay in a fixed position but the whole ladder gets higher. However, too high a fundamental and the perceived loudness of the upper harmonics will become difficult to distinguish, not to mention hard to produce from a physical point of view as the overtones get closer together. Conversely, a low fundamental means lots of 'head room' for the production of overtones, but too low and the formants produced are not conducive to the production of audible overtones. The voices of men and women can vary across a range from the highest note of a soprano at around 1000 Hz, down to a low male bass at about 80 Hz. The vocal structures of most people seem to favour a pitch between 180 – 300 Hz as the best point from which to produce clear overtones. This range equates to a spread across baritone, tenor and alto, and the start of soprano i.e. most people. The frequencies 180 – 300 Hz lie between the low F# and middle C on a piano.

A NOTE ABOUT BREATHING

In the West breathing tends to focus on the in-breath and the inflation of the chest. You will achieve more control over your voice if you adopt 'diaphragmatic' or 'belly' breathing. If you practice one of the many styles of yoga, the Buddhist 'pranayama' or other type of breath-focused meditation, or one of the many types of martial arts (T'ai Chi, Qigong, etc.) you may already be familiar with this technique.

To achieve this way of breathing sit in an upright, but relaxed, position. Place one hand on your stomach and one on your chest, now breathe in. If the hand on your chest moves out more than the one on your stomach do not be surprised. However, if the hand on your stomach moves out more then you are already breathing in this way.

Do this again and focus on the breath being drawn right down into the stomach so that this area gently inflates more than the chest. Do not overdo this or cause yourself discomfort and strain, all we are looking to do is bring the air into a much lower section of the lungs than is normally used. This process may be aided if you consciously use your stomach muscles to gently expel the air when you exhale. This ensures that the lungs are emptied efficiently and focuses the attention on the correct area for the following in breath. After exhaling, your stomach muscles should be nice and tight – let them go and air should automatically rush back in through your nose (with your mouth shut).

This may feel strange at first but breathing with the emphasis on the out breath carries many benefits. Using a gentle abdominal pressure on the out breath ensures that all stale air is expelled and allowing the in breath down into the belly means that fresh air is naturally drawn deep into the lungs. As this is more efficient the rate of breathing may naturally fall and a state of mental and physical relaxation may quickly follow. This style of breathing also directly strengthens the diaphragm and facilitates a greater lung capacity, both of which will allow better control over the voice. A longer sustain and more power can easily be achieved without strain, once this style of breathing becomes second nature.

Note:
Another excellent way to encourage this style of breathing and to strengthen the diaphragm is to learn to play the didjeridoo (Australian Aboriginal wind instrument). You may wish to seek out my other book; 'How to play the didjeridoo – a practical guide for everyone' ISBN 0-9539811-0-X.

WARM-UP EXERCISES

Some exercises for warming up prior to singing will help us to achieve better control and also ensure that strains and injury can be avoided. These exercises are designed to increase flexibility in the chest, back and shoulders and to allow the intercostals (spaces between the ribs) to soften. Proceed with care if you have any injury or history of problems in these areas.

Start by standing with feet shoulder-width apart and knees 'soft' or slightly bent, arms hanging loosely at your sides. Feel yourself connected to the earth through the soles of your feet. Slowly raise your arms above your head and then stretch your arms up from your shoulders as though trying to reach up for something then slowly lower them all the way back down to your sides. Next swing your torso from the hips, gently from side to side so that your loose arms swing around you. Do this for a minute or two. With your arms by your sides gently shrug your shoulders straight up and down, letting go all tension in the shoulders and upper back. Slowly reach down your left side with the left arm so that your waist bends slightly to the left, return and repeat on the other side. Using your left hand, massage your ribs on the right side then massage the left side with the right hand.

Try focusing your attention onto the breath for a few moments and use the 'belly' breathing mentioned earlier to bring the breath in deeply and expel old air from the lungs. This may make you yawn, if so go with it and really open your mouth wide. If not then open the mouth to trigger the yawn and really stretch the mouth and jaw.

Bring your hands up to your face and gently knead your face, particularly around the jaw joint so that this becomes relaxed and loose. Yawn again and really feel the throat opening and loosening. Stick your tongue out and try to touch your chin with it! Then try to touch your nose with your tongue. Do not be surprised if you do not get anywhere near in both cases, we are just looking to stretch the tongue. Now pull the tongue all the way back into the throat and then relax it again.

Draw in a breath deep into the belly and exhale in three breaths through an open mouth (but no vocal) – 'HUH HUH HUUUUUH'. The last exhalation should be extended for as long as you feel comfortable as the belly draws in to expel the air. This last exercise helps to strengthen the diaphragm and can be repeated up to three times. Do not overdo this however, especially if it makes you dizzy.

Now choose a comfortable pitch and start to hum with the mouth closed. Add a little pressure from the diaphragm and open the mouth into an 'AAHHH' sound. Try to project the sound across the room. Start off from a low pitch and slowly slide up in a glissando or 'siren sound' until you are as high as you feel comfortable. Do not worry if your voices 'breaks' at various points on the way up, just try to go as smoothly as you can. Come all the way back down again, if you need to pause for breath try to resume at the same pitch before continuing. Then try going gently up and down in one breath.

Your body and voice should now be nicely relaxed and ready to have fun!

'WESTERN' STYLE SINGING

Words in bold in the main text refer to sounds that can be found on the CD. The track number follows in brackets. Some sounds have their own tracks whilst others are one sound after the other, with obvious pauses, on one track. Listen to them as you move through the text, or at any time as a reminder (especially when you are practicing).

Take time to study the illustrations showing the mouth and tongue positions (you may wish to use a mirror to track your own mouth position). Read through the explanations until you are sure you understand them, and then try the various exercises whilst listening to the relevant portion of the CD. This process should ensure that you will achieve the various sounds with minimum effort. (No guarantees given however!).

THE BASIC SOUND

Sit or stand as you prefer but remain relaxed. With the mouth closed, draw in a good breath through the nose and start humming a note somewhere in the middle of your range. Leaving the jaw relaxed and the teeth slightly apart hum an 'mmm' sound. Focus your attention on your tongue – where is it in your mouth? Try flattening the tongue into its resting place in your lower jaw then arch it up so it is right up in the roof of your mouth. Hum and do this again slowly and listen to the way the sound changes – you may wish to block your ears and try this for better volume. The sound should move from a 'maaww' sound to more of a 'mmeee' sound. This change is you hearing overtones or harmonics. Now repeat the original 'mmm' hum, use some diaphragmatic pressure to give the sound volume and then start to drop your jaw whilst keeping your mouth closed. You could also try blocking your ears with your fingers and slowly moving your jaw up and down as far as you can whilst still keeping the lips together (keep the hum going). This should have a similar, if more subtle, effect. Hum again, add the extra pressure and keep your tongue in its low position (D5), but this time purse your closed lips and then open your mouth very slightly. The sound should immediately change to a soft **'mmoorr' (1)** sound. Whilst keeping this tone going slowly open the mouth wider and wider in a

CD track

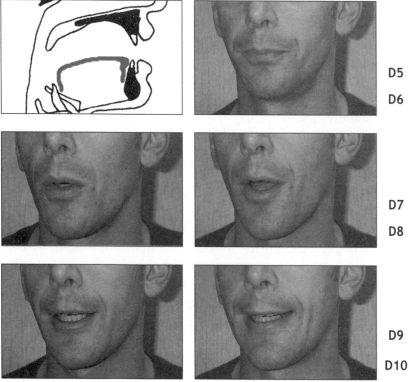

D5
D6

D7
D8

D9
D10

WESTERN STYLE SINGING   21

growing circle and, when you get quite wide, start to open out sideways into a wide smile. End up with a wide and narrow smile (of a kind!) so that the lips are quite close together again (D6 - 11).

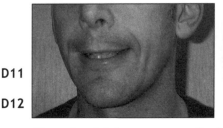

D11

D12

(2) You should hear a wonderful range of harmonics that move from 'mmooor' through something that sounds like **'mmoooaaarrrreeee' (2)**. Congratulations – you are singing with overtones! If you are finding these sounds hard to hear try the position shown in D12. With one hand cupped behind one ear use the other hand to direct the sound from the mouth back towards the other hand. This will really focus the sound into the ear and increase perceived volume. Try doing the previous range of sounds again whilst oscillating the size of the mouth slightly, then move to different positions randomly.

(3) Now try the hum with pursed lips and slowly open the mouth keeping the lips puckered outwards. As each overtone becomes audible keep that jaw / mouth position momentarily and try flexing the lips into a more or less exaggerated pucker or 'fish mouth' – this may help the overtones to become clearer and brighter. You could also try closing your mouth and opening into a **'mmmooooooo' (3)** sound, then close and open to a **'mmmooooorr' (3)**, then try **'mmmaaaah' (3), 'mmmiii' (3)** (pronounced my), **'mmmaaaay' (3)**, then finally **'mmmeeee' (3)** for the highest overtone. Sing the vowels 'a e i o u' whilst keeping the sound started by the 'a' (aye) and shaping the other vowels around this. In fact if we change the order to **'u o a i e' (4)** we can hear the ascending overtones.

(4)

Other ways to explore the foundations of overtones are; shape your mouth whilst using an **electric toothbrush (5)** or try flicking your **cheek (5)** with your fore finger, level with your back molar teeth, whilst shaping the mouth, see D13. If you can whistle you may wish to try whistling an ascending scale. Hear and feel how the tongue position changes the sound from low to high.

(5)

 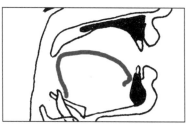

D13

D14

NASALITY

Whilst trying the previous section you may have been aware of how much of the sound travelled into your nasal cavities. This is an important part of overtone singing and can help reach the higher overtones and / or impart a different quality to the sound. Nasality is controlled by the structures at the back of the mouth, the tongue and the soft palette (velum) in particular. The raising of the back of the tongue, whilst simultaneously lowering the velum, sends more of the sound up into the sinuses (D14). The glottis also plays a part in this process - this is the flap that lies between the vocal cords which opens and closes the larynx. The consonant G (short harsh form not 'Jee') causes the closing of this structure and sends the tongue back and up so try saying 'gong' and feeling and hearing the effect. Say 'gong' and prolong the final sound 'ng' into a hum and hear how nasal it is. Now try doing it repeatedly so that you can feel the glottis opening and closing.

You could also try singing 'la' and prolong the 'ah' ending, then try with 'lung' and prolong the 'ng' into a sung tone. You should hear the difference immediately, it is much more nasal in quality. You can discover how much of this sound is exiting your nose by singing the 'lung' again and gently pinching the nostrils shut with your thumb and fore finger. The sound stops as soon as the nostrils are closed. Sing the following words and prolong the final consonant into a sung tone in each case: 'ging' 'gang' 'gong' 'gung'. This sequence should produce a series of descending overtones.

Try to ensure that the mouth shapes the words correctly and then run through the words forwards and back again ⑥ **'ging gang gong gung gong gang ging' (6)**. This technique is useful for finding rhythm in overtones as they are quite clearly defined by the glottal stop. Simple melodies can be easily created by repeating patterns made from these four nonsense words.

Try singing 'ging gong ging gong ging gong gang ging'. Now make up your own patterns.

'PISTON' TONGUE

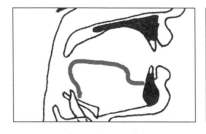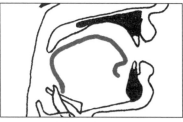

D15

D16

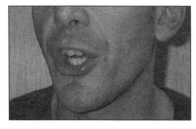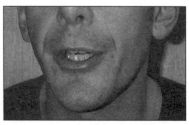

D17

D18

This may sound strange but you will see what I mean when you try it. It feels as if the tongue becomes a piston which moves to and fro in the cavity of the mouth to shape the sound. Start by gently pulling the tongue in so it is at the back of your mouth but try to keep it flat! Try pulling the front of the tongue in and then pulling the whole tongue back (D 15). This may feel a bit weird so try moving the tongue from this position to one all the way forward and touching the back of the teeth. This extreme forward and backward motion, if repeated, will build up flexibility and strength in the tongue.

Start to hum, somewhere in the middle of your vocal range. Shape the mouth into a gentle pucker and open it mid-way to produce a clear 'more' sound (D17). Move the tongue to the back position you have just tried (but not so far back as to be uncomfortable or close off the sound), the

sound will drop slightly in pitch and sound more like
(7) 'mmaaaww' (7). Next try moving the tongue forward
slowly whilst continuing the hum, you should produce
some clear **overtones (7)**.

Try this again, but this time go really slowly. The tongue
should start from low and back, moving to a position
forwards and arched up into the roof of your mouth
behind your teeth (D16). Then try it in reverse. Listen to
each overtone and rest a little on each one. Try adding a
little more pressure and changing the shape of the mouth
very slightly – listen out for a clearer tone. A subtle
change may cause an overtone to 'pop' out really clearly,
when it does try to stop at that position and really focus
the attention on the exact placement of mouth, tongue,
jaw, etc. As the tongue comes to a mid-way position on its
way forward start to raise it up as well as going forward
so that it arches up close to the roof of your mouth. Keep
the front pulled in (not easy I know) and only allow the
front to project out into an 'Eee' vowel as you get nearer
the back of the upper teeth. This last motion will trigger
some of the higher overtones. You may need to pull in the
sides of the mouth slightly to help the 'Eee' sound (D18).
Remember that the overtones get much closer together as
they go higher – this translates into 'harder to produce'.

You may also like to try making the sound more or less
(8) **nasal (8)** by raising the very back of your tongue as you
sing, this will cause some of the sound to exit through
your nasal cavities. The brain learns new skills by
repetition so keep trying this until you can really feel and
hear the overtones as distinct differences in pitch (but do
not alter the fundamental, which must remain constant).

You may start to tune into the subtleties of these sounds and once you do you may hear them everywhere. Listen to the sound of an airplane flying overhead or a vacuum cleaner being used – both of these sound sources are often rich in overtones / harmonics. Try tuning into each component of a sound, one at a time. Start humming a low tone and slowly bring the pitch up until you will hear, and probably feel, the hummed tone match that of the sound you are listening to – it starts to sound 'fuller'. If you move upwards from this pitch you will almost certainly find one or more other frequencies of the sound to resonate with. In this way you may hone your abilities to hear subtle differences in sound frequencies.

The eminent ear, nose and throat specialist Alfred Tomatis discovered that the human voice cannot recreate frequencies that are not heard (or recognised) by the ear / brain. He developed a unique apparatus called 'the listening ear' that allows the hearing process to be fine-tuned and certain deficiencies in the ability to perceive specific frequencies to be overcome. You can develop your own hearing abilities (without the aid of a 'listening ear') by producing and listening to your own overtones.

During your experimentation you may start to hear snatches of melodies or things that sound familiar – try making up your own simple melodies. Remember that the overtone series does not follow the Western scale so you will not be able to produce all the notes used in many popular melodies! Explore and discover your own tunes that are composed from the overtone series. **Track 9** (9) features a simple melody.

'CUPPED' TONGUE

This is a variation on the piston tongue technique that some people find easier. I, personally, find it easier to have more precise control of the overtones using this style. There is good evidence that this style allows higher overtones (up to the 20th harmonic) to be reached more easily, when compared with the 'piston' technique.

D19

D20

D21

D22

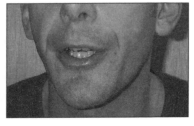

With the tongue laying in its rest position in the lower jaw try 'cupping' the tongue (i.e. curling up the sides and front) as though you were holding some liquid there (D19). Project a clear tone with the jaw dropped and a vocal like **'HORRRRE' (10)**. The tongue should be cupped low in the mouth, somewhat towards the back. Ensure that the mouth is open and the lips pursed into a medium sized 'O'. The first few **overtones (10)** are found by gently pursing the lips out further (D21), then start to bring the tongue up and forward very slowly. As this is happening the mouth should start to open a fraction

(10)

whilst the lips purse even more. Make sure the lips move only vertically into an exaggerated 'fish' mouth.

When you hear the overtones start to have an **'Rree' (11)** (11) component start to bring the jaw up slowly. As the tongue moves up towards the roof of the mouth it can start to flatten out or even arch up in its front half so that it is mimicking the curve of the roof of the mouth without actually making contact with it. When the middle of the tongue is very close to or touching the edge of the soft palette the sound should have moved into more of an **'Eeee' (11)** sound – the higher harmonics. Start to point (11) the front of the tongue but leave the front third cupped if you can (this is tricky but persevere). Now continue to push the tongue out from the back so that the cupped front part moves along parallel to the front upper palette but not actually touching it (D20). At the same time the mouth starts to widen into an 'E' pronunciation (D22).

The very highest overtones are hard to find but try bringing the teeth closer together and projecting the lower jaw slightly. At the same time purse the lips and move the cupped tongue tiny amounts to and fro, very close to the front part of the palette (but probably not touching it). This may sound like a nightmare to achieve but in reality the human mind / body has an amazing ability for bio-feedback – that is to focus into the sound and fine tune it by very small increments. Once you have done this exercise a few times try letting the body go and disengage the 'thinking' mind. Let yourself wander into the sound and see where it takes you. You might be surprised by the sounds that emerge!
Listen to **track 12** for inspiration. (12)

'POPPED' TONES

Once you feel comfortable with what you have learned and experienced so far you may wish to try other variations of 'Western' style singing. One of these I call 'popped' tones as it sounds as if the overtones 'pop' out at specific points along a hummed tone. You may remember the exercises on the harsh glottal sounds 'g' or 'ng'. This 'popped' technique uses a combination of a glottal stop, some nasality, and lip control. Try singing **'mung' 'mong'** (13) 'mang' 'ming' (13)** so that the nasal 'ng' sound is shuttered by the lips opening and closing on the next 'm' sound.

For a less nasal sound go back to the hummed 'mmooorrr' sound with the lips open and puckered. This time 'pop' the lips open and shut with the words **'mmoorr' 'mmooo'** (14) 'mmaaa' 'mmaayy'** and finally **'mmeee' (All 14)** for the highest tone. If you focus some attention on the tongue, so that this is used also, the sounds may become clearer. The tongue goes through positions similar to those in 'piston tongue' – low and back for the low tone and high arched and forward for the higher tones (D15, 16). This technique is used very fluently by Michael Vetter on many of his recordings (see Resources).

Both the 'piston' and 'cupped' styles of singing are used by many of the well-known overtone singers in the West; Michael Vetter, David Hykes, Rollin Rachele (mainly 'piston tongue'), Christian Bollman, Jim Cole and others.

See Resource section for suggested listening.

OTHER VARIANTS

Try inter-mixing parts from all of the Western styles. Starting from the low overtone (predominantly 'O' vowel position) try triggering the sounds from different consonants; H K L M N etc and see how this changes the sound.

You could also try the vocal 'fry'. This sounds alarming but it is simply vocalising a tone through very slack vocal cords. Children often unconsciously make this sound in play – it is like a croak or maybe the voice of the cartoon character 'Elmer Fudd'.

Try saying **'ER' (15)** whilst dropping the pressure right off and the tone should break into a soft croaking sound. Try 'switching' this sound on and off and then singing it in a protracted way whilst shaping the mouth and lips – this leads to some very soft and diffuse overtones that are similar to 'khöömei'.

(15)

'KHÖÖMEI' STYLE SINGING
INTRODUCTION AND WARNING

If you are just starting out with overtone singing and your interest (and perhaps a little impatience) has brought you straight to this section I wish to outline a caveat. The various styles of singing that originate in Central Asia are a good deal more difficult than the 'Western' styles and require some unusual vocal gymnastics. Throat singers from Mongolia and Tuva are taught from an early age so their bodies can adapt to these new skills. Unless you have worked thoroughly through the 'Western' section (and have a good degree of mastery of these styles) or have previously been taught the fundamentals of true khöömei singing I would warn against throwing yourself into the practical part of this section.

There are a few people who believe that this type of singing can cause bodily injury – I would say that this is only possible if proper care and consideration for warm-up and prior experience are disregarded. It is true that much of what makes khöömei so different will lead us into the realms of vocals that require more abdominal pressure, vocal constraint and precise control than may normally be used for conventional singing. However, I believe that a combination of adequate warm up, specific exercises and steady progression will allow us to experience this wonderful range of techniques without problems.

The absolute golden rules for all that follows are:

- Do not rush anything!
- Always take time to warm up the body and the voice before singing styles of khöömei
- Avoid food immediately prior to singing and ensure adequate water intake
- Do not do too much. Start with short sessions and increase slowly
- Do not attempt khöömei if you have a sore throat or cough, a cold or any other ailment that affects the tongue, throat, and lungs. Asthmatics need to

be extra careful but if they proceed slowly they may actually find many of the exercises beneficial.

• If you ever experience contra indications such as soreness in the throat, protracted coughing, or feeling dizzy – STOP. Take a few days off and be extra careful when you try again.

AIR LOCKS AND SQUEEZING

Strange names for some strange techniques. One of the prerequisites for good khöömei singing lies in the ability to have strict control of the flow of air from the lungs, through the vocal cords and the glottis, and out of the mouth. We have looked previously at diaphragmatic breathing and abdominal pressure. Hopefully you will now be familiar with the concept of applying solid inwards and downwards pressure in the abdomen to assist the projection of more power and volume through the vocals. This process is not fully understood but most will be familiar with the need to 'bear down' when voiding the bowels i.e. 'having a poo' (sorry). This action causes the diaphragm to exert pressure on the lungs, forcing out more air. In addition a tightening or 'locking' occurs somewhere in the upper abdomen that creates back-pressure so that the air exiting from the lungs is under greater pressure and is controlled to allow slower release.

Try **vocalising (16)** a tone whilst applying this pressure ⟨16⟩ gently. At first it may constrict the throat as well, and choke off the sound into a grunt, but keep the throat relaxed and open so that the pressure just makes the volume increase markedly. Try an exaggerated laugh 'HA HA HA' for the same trigger in the belly.

Using the diaphragm 'lock' technique we can build considerable pressure in the air exiting the lungs but we need to control it by also squeezing in the throat so we can make the sound last. This squeezing technique is one of the hardest parts of khöömei to master so some perseverance will be needed. What we are looking to do is create a very specific squeeze or constriction right above the vocal folds (it is quite likely that a tightening of the folds themselves also occurs).

If you are a classically trained singer you will probably recoil in horror at the thought of this and the resultant sound. However, as long as due care is given to warm-up and this technique is tried a little at a time there is no evidence that this technique causes any problems with either conventional singing practices or any part of the vocal physiology.

If you tried the vocal 'fry' technique in the previous chapter then it gives some insight into the characteristics of this sound and how it is produced. Two ways of focusing in on the specific sound that have worked, with some hilarity, in workshops I have led are; do an impression of a lamb or goat with their 'Baa' (pronounced 'Bear') or try saying 'Tony Blair' whilst sticking your tongue right out on the **'Blair' (17)**. You may start to hear a high-speed croak or buzzing component and this is what we are looking for.

If you do not see (or rather hear) what I mean borrow a

dry electric shaver. Hold it against your throat, to the side of your voice box, and switch it on. If you open your mouth you should be presented with a most alarming buzzing sound, shaping your mouth with the unspoken vowels 'A E I O U' will produce some great overtones. Other models of this sound are the Daleks from TV's Dr. Who (UK), Wolfman Jack the 50's US DJ, or Ned the Vietnam Vet in the TV cartoon South Park.

Listen to the sound samples on the CD and mimic them until you can produce this sound without coughing or producing strain in any part of the larynx / throat. Try to localise the 'squeeze' component to a very thin plane across, and just above, the vocal cords. For men this point lies almost directly across the top of the Adam's Apple. Women will need to use fore finger and thumb to gently squeeze the exterior throat to find the vertical ring-like structures of the trachea, count down three from the top and this should be where the squeezed vocal needs to be triggered. Practice until it sounds like **this (18)**. The sound should be almost 'metallic' in quality and when your throat is open and relaxed (apart from the squeeze – contradictory I know) you should be able to sustain it for quite some time.

(18)

KHÖÖMEI

Although this name is used as a 'catch-all' for the many styles of Central Asian throat singing, it is also a specific style. Khöömei is characterised by soft, floaty, harmonics. It features similarities with some Western styles in that the harmonics can be shaped with the mouth more directly as well as with the tongue. It is often triggered from a 'HOO' vocal with many of the same physical positions as 'cupped' tongue in Western style.

The slightly hollowed tongue moves through small

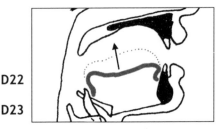

D22

D23

amounts in a vertical direction from the base position in the lower jaw (D22) whilst the main sounds are shaped by the mouth / lips. Follow the mouth shapes shown in D7 - D11. Experiment by using a slight flexing of the lips into a pucker to help shape the sounds (D23). The first few overtones are to be found in the very subtle changes in mouth shape at this early stage, a slight flex of the lips may be enough.

The main difference between the khöömei voice and the Western style is the introduction of the 'squeezed voice' technique mentioned previously. With the trigger of the squeeze (which the Mongolians call *shahalttai*) the 'Hoo' is more akin to saying the word **'WHOOOOO'**. Listen to **(19)** for an example that starts as a steady fundamental then goes up and back down. Track 19 also features a short **melody** sung in khöömei style.

The Mongolian singers use their own vowel sounds to trigger the harmonics in khöömei so you may wish to try these. They are: *ü* as the 'o' in 'who', *u* as the 'ou' in 'source', *ö* as the 'o' in 'money', *o* as the 'o' in the English 'hot', *i* as the 'i' in 'tin', *e* as the 'e' as in 'den', and *a* as the 'u' in 'but'. Some of these feature very subtle differences.

SYGYT

This style is harder to achieve than straight khöömei but the resultant sounds are worth the effort! This style is the one that seems to have caught a lot of attention in the West as it sounds very flute-like and 'non-human'. Sygyt (or sigit) translates as 'whistle' and this style is characterised by a high-pitch whistling overtone. The downside is that this technique employs quite considerable internal pressure so please proceed with caution.

Start with a hummed 'MMM' that has plenty of volume and diaphragm pressure. Before you open your mouth place the tip of your tongue up against your palette, somewhere between the back of your upper teeth and the beginning of the higher palette. Your teeth should be just apart and as you open your mouth add some **'Errr' (20)** (20) sound and bring the lower jaw forward slightly (D 24). The lips should not be opened too much and have a slight pursed shape. The position of the tongue should define an 'L' sound i.e. with the tip up against the forward hard palette and the body of the tongue sloping back down towards the root of the tongue (D 25). Now apply a little throat squeeze (see Airlocks and Squeezing) which should define the sound and cause the area of the exterior throat directly below and either side of the chin to tighten slightly. All being well you should be treated to some strong clear and almost piercing **overtones (21)**. If not, (21) do not worry. Try gently and subtly changing each main component of jaw, mouth, lips, tongue, etc until the clear tones pop out. Remember, the tongue should be up at the front and down at the back.

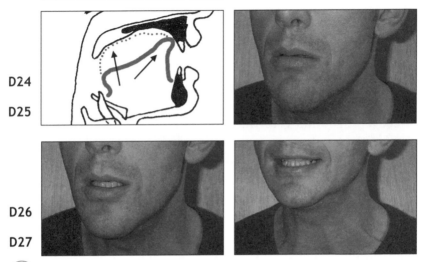

D24

D25

D26

D27

(22) The higher **overtones (22)** are achieved by pushing forward from the root of the tongue and flexing the body of the tongue up into the higher palette whilst keeping the tip and front part of the tongue lightly cupped in the same spot on the front palette (D 24). The mouth shape should follow D 25 - D 27. Note the forward jutting jaw in D 26 and the supporting tension in the neck in D 27.

Some singers prefer to create this style with a tongue that lifts up and forward so that it becomes cupped and touches the upper front teeth and molars all the way around. Obviously this position leaves no aperture for the sound to escape so you will need to experiment by creating a small gap somewhere along the interface between teeth and tongue. The main positions used by many singers are: flexing the tongue slightly so that it leaves a small gap between the tongue and the teeth at the very front, or twisting the tongue a little to pull the front third away from the incisors slightly on the left or right.

The tongue and throat gymnastics used in Sygyt take a while to get used to so do not be unduly worried if your throat feels a little tight after this. The muscles of the throat and tongue need to adapt and get stronger / more flexible and also the vocal cords need to acclimatise. The occasional tickle, scratchy sensation, or short cough is all part of the process of allowing the vocal cords, and the muscles that support them, to gain strength. Any other signs of strain or discomfort should be heeded and you may need to leave this technique alone for a while. Sipping water, warm herbal tea or gargling with an infusion of sage will all help support your body in this new adventure. Listen to track 23 for a short demonstration of **Sygyt**.

(23)

KARGYRAA

Kargyraa (spellings vary) is quite similar to the Tibetan low chant and as such is about the most outlandish sound that the human voice can create. On first hearing kargyraa many people react with disbelief and even experience physical effects like shaking or shivering. There is something very primal about this sound as it reaches very low frequencies that can be anything down to two octaves below an individual's normal vocal range. It is hard to produce and even harder to control and requires care and attention if vocal irritation is to be avoided. The rough translation of kargyraa is 'to expectorate' – to clear one's throat. A note to women; there has been a good deal of quite sexist assumptions that women are unable to learn to throat sing. This is completely unfounded and women can produce beautiful overtones in all the styles. However, I will say that kargyraa requires the triggering of lower vocal frequencies that are not evident in many women's vocal ranges. It is possible for women to learn this style, and when they do it has a quality quite unlike the male version, but women will find it harder and must protect against strain to the vocal cords.

The trigger of the sound for this style comes from the voice but this is merely that, a trigger, and the vibration should quickly move to the so-called 'false' vocal cords as the exciter (thing which produces the vibration). These are small flaps or folds that occur in the larynx just above and below the voice box. Moving the resonance to these early on means that there should be no vocal strain in this style, in fact to achieve good kargyraa the whole chest cavity, the larynx and throat must be open and relaxed. The sound should quickly find resonance in the chest, particularly behind the breast bone so place your hand there and visualise the sound moving down into your chest until you can feel the vibration quite clearly with your hand.

(24) Start with the mouth closed and cough or clear the **throat (24)**. Listen to the vibrations coming from the vocal folds / throat and try to move this sound down into the **chest (24)** as though you had a chesty cold. Ideally you should be able to feel the vibrations through your breastbone – remember to keep your hand there. Now

bring the sound of the clearing of the throat higher up in the throat. Think of a cough you might make to attract attention if you were being ignored!

Listen out for the more nasal components of this sound and, employing a little of the throat squeeze, try to elongate the final part of this cough into a 'rumbling buzz'. This will need a good deal of support from the diaphragm and a little pressure in the muscles of the neck, but no strain or pressure in the vocal cords. Listen again for, and encourage, the nasal components – the sound **sample (25)** is the kargyraa sound triggered with the mouth closed and moved from nasal to chest resonance. Once you have established this nasal sound try pushing the tongue forward until it is against the back of the lower teeth and arched slightly in the lower jaw space (D 28). Now open your mouth and let the sound out into a **'MMHOORRAAAGGHH' (25)** (D 29).

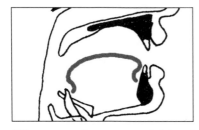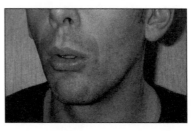

D28

D29

The sound may quickly lose itself into a stuttering exhalation and / or make the throat feel sore and even cause you to cough a little. Take some sips of water and gently try again. Once you can project this sound for a little while, say 5 seconds or so, try to visualise the throat relaxing and opening. This may seem at odds with what you are doing but, as explained previously, once this sound is triggered and held in the right way it should provide no strain for the vocal cords or the throat. It is thought that this sound is in fact the false vocal folds, and other nearby structures, resonating instead of the vocal cords. Keep practicing (though not too much or too often – try other easier styles instead) and aim to bring the sound down into the chest or belly. This can only be achieved by relaxing but it brings all the deepest notes – those that might be termed 'sub-harmonics' as they are vibrating at frequencies below that of the fundamental. As some men can have vocal ranges that extend as low as 80 Hz, harmonics may be possible down to 40Hz.

After a good deal of practice you will be able to sustain the kargyraa for half a minute or more, with good pressure and nice relaxed quality. The next stage is to shape the sound by opening the mouth into the sounds **'URGH'** **'OH' 'AH' 'AYY' 'EYE' 'EEE' (26)** which correspond with the ascending overtones or harmonics. The harmonics in this style are shaped in a similar way to khöömei – with the mouth aperture which should move from an open 'O' to a wide and quite closed 'E' shape (D7 - D11). The higher overtones, in particular, may be hard to achieve without good supporting pressure and the tongue being firmly 'locked' in place in the lower jaw.

The possible overtones, like all overtone singing, are directly related to the pitch of the fundamental (the hummed or sung note). With kargyraa the overtones are more like 'undertones' or sub-harmonics as they are lower than the fundamental. Therefore the lower you can get your normal singing voice the lower your kargyraa will be. Those with larger chests may experience the wonderful super-deep tones so favoured by the Mongolian and Tuvan singers. Women, with their higher vocal register, will (of course) not be able to go as low as most men. Nonetheless they will still be capable of producing harmonics well below their normal range. Realising this goal and singing kargyraa has been an empowering experience for most women I know who have achieved it.

OTHER VARIANTS

There are many other sub-styles and divisions of khöömei style singing - a few are listed below:

Tibetan 'low-voice'. This style takes the monks many (27) years to perfect and is a very complex set of sounds. Something similar can be achieved by attempting kargyraa with a very open throat and softer trigger for the voice that is more like a soft breathy **'HOOOOOO'** **(27)** sound with lots of diaphragm pressure to keep the air flow up. The tongue is kept loose and low in the jaw, do not lock it against the lower teeth as with kargyraa. **Track 27** <u>mimics</u> the sound and vowel shapes used by the monks when chanting their mantras - see the Resource section for suggested listening of the real thing.

Borbangnadyr (or borbannadir). Means 'rolling' and is (28) very akin to standard khöömei with a squeezed voice but uses fast tremolos and trills of the tongue and lips. Sing with a khöömei voice but try to oscillate the tongue through small movements in a vertical direction to create the warbling effect. Flexing the lips very slightly to make them 'quiver' also helps this style to emerge. The Tuvans use this style to invoke the naturalistic sounds of running water, birds, etc. **Track 28** features a short sample of this style.

(29) **Dumchuktaar**. Means 'nose' or 'from the nose' and is used to describe any of the khöömei styles when sung through the nose with the mouth closed. Try it – it is good for practicing as it is only loud in the singer's head! Listen carefully to **track 29** for my example.

(30) **Ezengileer**. Derived from the name for 'stirrup'. This technique requires a khöömei voice with squeeze that has rhythmic oscillations that are meant to sound like a horse galloping and also the clinking of the metal stirrups. This oscillation is accomplished by rapidly opening and closing the glottis – remember the 'NGN' trigger sound in the Western section. The 'clinking' sound that is supposed to mimic that of the metal stirrups is sometimes added by tapping a bowl or similar whilst singing but some singers manage it by producing very short and high overtones (this is quite rare!). **Track 30** features my version of this style.

ADVANCED EXERCISES AND FURTHER SUGGESTIONS

Learning to sing many of the forms of throat singing well can takes years and is really an on-going journey in search of the 'perfect' sounds. Once you feel you have gained sufficient control of the various styles you may wish to try the following advanced exercises to explore these wonderful singing techniques further.

Learning to count overtones.

Hopefully by now you will have gained many weeks experience singing in one or many of the different styles and have attuned your hearing to the subtle sounds of harmonics. Choose a singing style you are comfortable with and, singing with a mid-range fundamental, start with the very first overtone you can hear. This will be with a mouth position very close to that in which you started. If you are singing in a style that uses mouth shape to create overtones (Western 'basic', khöömei, kargyraa) this means you may need to only flex your lips slightly from the smallish 'O' mouth shape that you began with. If you are singing in a style that utilises tongue positions for overtone production ('cupped' tongue, Sygyt) you will need to move your tongue through a series of very small adjustments. Move backwards and forwards with very tiny alterations until you are sure that you can hear a difference between the starting fundamental and the harmonic you can hear first. All being well this will be the 2nd harmonic or the first overtone.

Proceed to raise the overtone to a higher pitch but go as slowly as you possibly can. Any movement that you have learnt to make to trigger overtones will need to be made slowly and methodically whilst listening for the next harmonic. When you hear the next change in overtone pitch consciously note the positions of all relevant structures; lips, tongue, jaw, etc. Now move on and listen out for the next change, and then the next. In this way you will become familiar with the process that links vocal 'posture' and position with the ascending overtones. Start over again and mentally count the overtones from one upwards as you ascend the scale. You should be able to count up into double figures but remember that those higher overtones are much harder to locate and emphasise. Listen to **(31)** for an idea of the progression of the overtones.

(31)

(32) **Fixed overtone with a changing fundamental.**
Choose a pitch and start singing. Once you have isolated a clear overtone, 'tune' into it and hear how it sounds. Now try moving the fundamental pitch up or down but come back to the previous harmonic as quickly as possible. You may remember that, in the theory section, we looked at the way the overtone series is made up of a sequence of harmonics that are in a fixed relationship to the fundamental. If the fundamental raises in pitch the harmonics raise with it, whilst keeping their relative positions from the fundamental. This exercise helps you to get better at identifying the overtone you are creating and improves your ability to find the same overtone again with an altered fundamental.

(33) **Rising fundamental and overtone together.**
Sing at a pitch somewhere in the lower part of your range and start with a lower harmonic. Now raise the fundamental pitch at the same time as moving the harmonics up. If this feels a little tricky try moving the overtones from a fixed pitch fundamental, as you will have done whilst working through this book. Next sing a rising pitch with your normal singing voice (no overtones). Combine the two so that you achieve the goal of both fundamental and overtone raising together, then come back down again. This should sound like a siren with overtones.

Rising fundamental and lowering overtone. (34)
This is similar to the previous exercise, the only difference being that the overtones come down in pitch whilst the fundamental goes up. This is a good deal more difficult. Try to trigger a clear high overtone from a low fundamental and concentrate on the pitch of your voice going up whilst simultaneously moving your tongue back down into the lower overtone position.

Lowering fundamental and rising overtone. (35)
This time start with a high pitch fundamental and a low overtone. Sing whilst lowering the fundamental but raising the overtone. Once again, concentrate on your voice so that it lowers in pitch whilst ensuring that your tongue moves up and forward to produce the higher overtones. This, and the previous technique, may need a good deal of practice before they gain a smooth flow.

Rhythm and timing. (36)
If you already have experience with creating music, maybe via conventional singing or instruments, you may have knowledge of rhythm and timing and how to bring it into your throat singing. For those less familiar with these terms this is simply the perceived 'pace' of the music, whether fast or slow. Most western music follows a regular structure or rhythm that doesn't change too often within one 'song' so that we find ourselves tapping our foot along with the beat. Although some types of music feature a little fluidity in timing most of us will be able to hear if a sound is made out of time as it just sounds 'wrong'. If you feel confident in your abilities to keep musical 'time' then you could try something as simple as tapping your finger on a table edge in a regular

beat whilst singing along. Try to ensure that any changes in note or overtone happen 'on' or 'off' a beat, that is to say as your finger hits the table or when it is at it's highest position before coming back down to hit the table again. You will hear the effect if it is 'out'. Start off singing along to slower beats and speed up as you gain confidence and skill. If you are not confident of your abilities to hold time you could try an electronic metronome. These can be bought from music shops, cost around £20 and produce a regular audible 'click' to follow.

(37) Altering loudness and pressure

By altering how much abdominal pressure is applied whilst singing we can change the perceived loudness of the resultant overtones. You will find that raising and lowering the pressure whilst singing a melody in overtones can really add to the expression of emotion in the sound. Try backing the pressure right off and let the sound tail off in volume and then raising the volume slightly, this can create quite a lonely sound reminiscent of the loneliness of the nomadic sheep herders who sing whilst in the mountains. Conversely, ramping the pressure up and increasing the volume can be very stimulating and uplifting. Try incorporating these elements into your singing and see how they affect the mood of the song.

(38) 'Flipping' the lips

This effect is produced by using a forefinger to 'flip' the lower lip whilst singing. The finger is held horizontally in front of the mouth and produces a short downward flick of the lip so that it is pulled a small distance downward before tension returns it to the starting position (D30 -

D30

D31

D31). This movement alters the pitch of the overtone and can be used rhythmically to great effect. You can also 'flip' both lips by oscillating the finger in front of the mouth so that both lips are 'flipped'. A combination of the khöömei style voice with this technique produces the sort of rhythmic sounds associated with the jaw harp (small metal instrument with a springy tang that is played in the mouth, between the teeth).

Tongue flip

(39)

I have never heard this used by anyone throat singing so I am going to take the rather bold step of claiming it as my own invention! (Please feel free to contradict me).

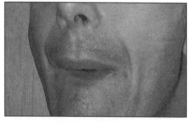

D32

Open the mouth and drop the lower jaw slightly whilst using the muscles of the lips to pull the lower lip into the mouth and over the lower teeth (D32). The lower lip should now be creating a 'cover' over the lower front teeth that comes someway into the mouth. If you hold this position whilst using the tip of the tongue to apply a rapid downward flick of the edge of the lower lip you should create a short 'popping' sound as the lip springs back.

With practice you will find that you can achieve this effect whilst singing at the same time. Obviously you will be limited to singing styles that do not need the tongue too much, khöömei is probably the easiest style to use.

(39) **Track 39** features a sample of this style.

(40) ## Accompaniment (instrumental)

Overtone singing sounds wonderful when accompanied by other musical instruments. Didjeridoos, tamboras, and harmoniums all produce continuous 'drone' sounds that are very relaxing to listen to. This drone also gives a pitch to harmonise with and if this pitch is matched by the sung fundamental then this becomes masked so that the overtones seem more prominent. The didjeridoo will need to be played by someone else but the tambora and harmonium are played with the hands so it is possible to play and sing simultaneously.

No melodies are necessary in accompaniment, which makes things easier if you are not familiar with any of these instruments. Once a degree of skill in reaching the desired overtones is achieved you may enjoy singing along to many other, more traditional, melodic instruments; cello, flute, piano, etc. However, remember that the overtone series and the classical Western scale do not follow one another so care will be needed to allow the throat singing to harmonise with the other (40) instruments. **Track 40** features free-form melodies with didjeridoo and then harmonium.

If you feel inspired to sing melodies in the style of the Tuvans and Mongolians you could ask friends to accompany you with instruments such as the jaw harp, the cello or viola (similar to the Morin Huur and Igil –

strung instruments bowed with horse hair), whistles or recorders, and small hand drums. See the Resource section for suggested listening.

Accompaniment (human)   (41)

Up to this point you may have explored throat singing by yourself as it is a wonderful journey of self-discovery. If you know others who might be interested in these sort of vocal gymnastics you may wish to enjoy the wonders of overtones from more than one voice – the results can be really quite magical. Group singing opens up all sorts of possibilities for harmonies and melodies and, as the overtone series is constructed of what I would term 'pure' sounds, you will find that most combinations sound tuneful. This exploration can be very liberating as you explore your voices without concern for musical scales or theory overmuch.

Group throat singing seems to becoming more popular with several urban areas advertising a 'toning group' or an 'overtone choir'. Do not be put off from attending such a group. It is normal to perhaps judge one's abilities or doubt that one has the necessary skills – do not doubt. I guarantee that there will be people in the group with less experience than yourself and all can participate with a sense of shared joy. If you have anyone in the group that has knowledge of music theory you may wish to explore specific intervals together, try 3rds and 5ths for example. **Track 41** features two singers together. (Actually myself twice thanks to computer technology!).

Environment   (42)

You may have already discovered that the perceived

quality of your overtones can be affected by your surroundings. Due to the nature of acoustics, harmonics are enhanced by very reflective surfaces. I mean that in an acoustic sense. Tiled floors and walls that bounce sound around and enhance the audibility of the higher harmonics, rather than heavy carpets and curtains which tend to 'swallow' the sound and render overtones less audible. Seek out tiled bathrooms, churches, corridors, stairwells, pedestrian tunnels, etc. These places will allow you to hear all the subtleties of your singing and are great for trying the fine tuning required to achieve the higher overtones. Track 42 features some throat singing recorded in the resonant space of a church.

(43) Look out for the bonus track 'Weak Hazy Sun' (43).

With practice, you will find that it is perfectly possible to practice singing whilst walking, driving, or riding a bicycle. In a city or town environment traffic noise is a good cover for some hearty kargyraa! I also discovered that practicing some of the khöömei styles in public is a great way of getting a seat on the bus or train – some people seem to worry when faced with a person making unusual sounds!

I sincerely hope that this book has been useful in your journey into the wonderful world of harmonics. If you discover any unusual sounds in your endeavours, wish to share comments about the book – or even a criticism, please feel free to e-mail me at the following address: Info@soundforhealth.com

BIBLIOGRAPHY AND RESOURCES

Books

There are not many books specifically about throat singing and even these are often hard to find or out of print. However, I heartily recommend the following and used them all extensively during my learning process.

D'Angelo, James. *Healing with the Voice.* Thorsons, London 2000.
Wonderful collection of exercises designed to heal via the voice, contains lots of information about overtones and harmonics and basic practical information.

Goldman, Jonathan. *Healing Sounds, The Power of Harmonics.* Inner Traditions, Vermont, USA 2002.
Excellent and thorough book on the healing aspects of sound but also has good sections on overtone singing with some practical explanation.

Leighton, R. *Tuva or Bust!.* WW Norton 1991.
No practical information but a great story about trying to get to Tuva.

Rachele, Rollin. *Overtone singing study guide.*
Cryptic Voices, Amderstam 1996.
Out-of-print and hard to find. Has excellent CD based exercises and lots of information but is pretty heavy on musical theory and a lot of staff notation – great if you can read music.

van Tongeren, Mark C. *Overtone Singing.* Fusica, Amsterdam 2002.

Very comprehensive study of the whole world of overtone singing that comes with an excellent CD featuring many examples of styles. Little practical explanation given.

The Web

Internet addresses are often liable to change so a search for the words 'khoomei, overtone singing, or throat singing' via Google will turn up lots of information. Here are a few good sites worth a visit:

www.soundforhealth.com
> Workshops and tuition in overtone singing, didjeridoo, Tibetan bowls, crystal bowls, chants & mantras, etc with Jonathan Cope.

www.healingsounds.com/
> Jonathan Goldman's site with information on the healing aspects of sound.

www.fotuva.org
> The Friends of Tuva, great info.

www.huunhuurtu.com
> The Tuvan musicians site.

www.scs-intl.com/trader/
> Tuvan music shopping site

www.tranquanghai.net/Websites_on_Overtones.html -
> Tran Quang Hai's site.

www.oberton.org
> German overtone site.

www.soundtransformations.btinternet.co.uk
> Michael Ormiston's site – lots of links.

www.healingvoice.com/
> Jill Purce's site.

www.fusica.nl/
    Marc Van Tongeren's site.
www.spectralvoices.com/
    Jim Cole and the Spectral Choir.
www.khoomei.com/
    The excellent site by Steve Sklar.
groups.yahoo.com/group/tuvanthroatsinging/
    Yahoo discussion group.
www.harmonicsounds.com/
    Nestor Kornblum and Michele Everard.
www.lichthaus-musik.de/
    Christian Bollman.
www.harmonicworld.com/
    David Hykes - one of the early pioneers.
www.sacredsound.net/
    Lyz Cooper and BAST.
asahi-net.or.jp/~XF3K-MKGM/index-e.html
    Japanese Khoomei society
www.yat-kha.com/
    Tuvan rock musicians - check Albert's voice!
www.ondar.com/
    Tuvan master throat singer.

Compact Discs

Tuva: Voices from the Centre of Asia.
    Smithsonian Folkways. Excellent recordings of
    many styles with lots of notes.

Michael Ormiston: *Winds of Heaven*
    Excellent UK khöömei singer.

Huun Huur Tu: *Where Young Grass Grows.*
Shanachie. Fantastic Tuvan traditional and
original compositions.

David Hykes: *Hearing Solar Winds.* Ocora.
Stunningly meditative Western style.

Egschiglen: *Sounds of Mongolia.* Arc Music.
Great collection of khöömei styles.

Jim Cole: *Sky.* Spectral Spiral Music.
Beautiful harmonies in Western style.

Yat Kha: *Aldyn Dashka.*
Mix of folk and rock with amazing styles of
khöömei.

The Spirit of the Steppes. Nascente.
Great collection of khöömei.

Sainkho Namtchylak: *Stepmother City.* Enisai.
Excellent female singer, quite avant-garde.

Shu-De: Voices from the Distant Steppe
Realworld/WOMAD Productions

Marc Van Tongeren. *Paraphony.* Fusica
Very nice melodies.

Deep in the Heart of Tuva. Ellipsis Arts.
Great collection with small informative book.

Jonathan Cope: Look out for my new CD, due out soon...

ABOUT THE AUTHOR

Jonathan Cope drove his parents to distraction when, as a child, he continually made 'funny' noises, whistled, and hummed or droned along with the vacuum cleaner. Luckily he was not put off by people's reactions and has continued through life being fascinated by all sorts of odd noises. Early in the 1990's he took up playing the didjeridoo. This instrument has led Jonathan through a wonderful series of adventures which have culminated in him teaching and leading workshops in the uses of sound for personal development and growth. Jonathan has been blessed with teachings received from many leaders in this field including; Jonathan Goldman, Chris James, Nestor Kornblum, Lyz Cooper, Michael Ormiston, Tserendavaa, Rollin Rachele, Djalu Gurriwirri, and Jill Purce amongst others.

Jonathan is currently available for tuition in all styles of throat singing, along with many other instruments and techniques in the field of sacred sound. He also leads regular workshops – see details on the website at: http://www.soundforhealth.com or e-mail for information at: info@soundforhealth.com

Jonathan Cope is also the author of the best-selling series *'How to Play the Didjeridoo'* in book and CD formats, available in stores or via the website.

Jonathan lives in London with his wife and son but travels to wherever sound carries him.

The author wishes to assert that this book was born from a sincere attempt to help share these wonderful techniques with others and that any factual mistakes contain herein are solely his responsibility. He hopes that you will not think less of him for any errors that may have crept in.

ACKNOWLEDGMENTS

I would like to extend sincere thanks and gratitude to all those wonderful teachers mentioned in 'About the author' for their sharing of wisdom and knowledge. Additionally I would also like to send thanks and love to my parents for help and encouragement, my wife Rosie similarly – hearing someone learn to throat sing is an act of supreme tolerance!

Big thanks also to: Tony Palmer and Jeremy Cope for Beta-testing, Rosie Brown for proof-reading and photography, Kyle Maplesden, Colin Simenksi, Steve Lawson, Sean Farrenden, Bear, Derek Furlong, Rami, and all those who have taken time to share energy with me – whether by attending one of my workshops or helping me with my understanding of the complex nature of sound and life!

And last, but not least, all those wonderful beings who shared so deeply with me at Sound Intensive 2003 and also throughout BAST training 2003 – I think of you all often.

OM AH HUM.

soundforhealth.com

Sound For Health leads regular workshops in the field of sacred sound. Subjects include: overtone singing, didjeridoo, Tibetan bowls, crystal bowls, chants & mantras, gongs, drums, etc. See the website for details.

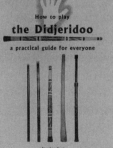

NOTES